MOHAN-MĀLĀ

(A GANDHIAN ROSARY)

BEING A THOUGHT FOR EACH DAY OF THE YEAR GLEANED
FROM THE WRITINGS AND SPEECHES OF MAHATMA GANDHI

COMPILED BY
R. K. PRABHU

D0835065

NAVAJIVAN PUBLISHING HOUSE
AHMEDABAD-380 014

Rupees Twenty-five

© Navajivan Trust, 1949

First Published, 30th January 1949
Second Revised Edition, 10,000 Copies,
January 1959
This Reprint, 3,000 Copies, January 2013
Total : 88,000 Copies

ISBN 978-81-7229-059-7

Printed and Published by
Vivek Jitendrabhai Desai
Navajivan Publishing House
Ahmedabad-380 014
INDIA

Phone : 079 - 27540635, 27542634
E-mail : jitnavjivan10@gmail.com
Website : www.navajivantrust.org

PREFACE

In this work I have essayed to present to the reader the essence of Mahatma Gandhiji's philosophy of life in the form of a Rosary of 366 "Pearls of Thought"— one "Pearl" for each day of the year, including the leap year—all gleaned from his writings and speeches. The "Pearls" have been so arranged as to make the transition from one thought to the next as smooth as possible, thus enabling the reader to make use of the *Rosary* either for daily contemplation of the given thought or for continuous reading at a stretch.

R. K. P.

PREFACE

TO THE READER

I would like to say to the diligent reader of my writings and to others who are interested in them that I am not at all concerned with appearing to be consistent. In my search after Truth I have discarded many ideas and learnt many new things. Old as I am in age, I have no feeling that I have ceased to grow inwardly or that my growth will stop at the dissolution of the flesh. What I am concerned with is my readiness to obey the call of Truth, my God, from moment to moment, and, therefore, when anybody finds any inconsistency between any two writings of mine, if he has still faith in my sanity, he would do well to choose the later of the two on the same subject.

M. K. GANDHI

Harijan, 29-4-1933, p. 2

SOURCES

BC   *The Bombay Chronicle*, daily newspaper published in Bombay.

DD   *Delhi Diary* (Prayer Speeches from 10-9-'47 to 29-1-'48), M. K. Gandhi, Navajivan Publishing House, Ahmedabad, 1948.

EF   *The Epic Fast*, by Pyarelal. Mohanlal Maganlal Bhat, Ahmedabad, 1932.

ER   *Ethical Religion*, by Mahatma Gandhi. S. Ganesan, Madras, 1930.

GIV   *Gandhiji In Indian Villages*, by Mahadev Desai. S. Ganesan, Madras, 1927.

H   *Harijan*, weekly journal edited by Gandhiji and others and published at Ahmedabad.

HS   *Hind Swaraj Or Indian Home Rule*, by Mahatma Gandhi. Navajivan Press, Ahmedabad, 1928.

LG   *Lenin and Gandhi*, by Rene Fullop-Miller. Putnam, London, 1930.

Auto   *The Story of My Experiments with Truth*, by M. K. Gandhi. Navajivan Press, Ahmedabad, 1956.

SRSI   *Self-Restraint v. Self-Indulgence*, by M. K. Gandhi. Navajivan Press, Ahmedabad, Pt. I (1930) and Pt. II (1939).

SSA   *Satyagraha in South Africa*, by M. K. Gandhi. Navajivan Press, Ahmedabad, 1928.

SW   *Speeches and Writings of Mahatma Gandhi*, G. A. Natesan, Madras, 4th Edition, 1933.

TI   *The Times of India*, daily Newspaper published in Bombay.

WGC   *With Gandhiji in Ceylon*, by Mahadev Desai. S. Ganesan, Madras, 1928.

YI   *Young India*, weekly journal edited by Gandhiji and published at Ahmedabad; ceased publication in February 1932.

YM   *From Yeravda Mandir*, by M. K. Gandhi. Navajivan Press, Ahmedabad, 2nd Edition, 1935.

MOHAN-MĀLĀ

JANUARY

And is this Power benevolent or malevolent? see it is purely benevolent. For
I can see that in the midst of death life

JANUARY 1

There is an indefinable mysterious Power that pervades everything. I feel it though I do not see it. It is this unseen Power which makes itself felt and yet defies all proof, because it is so unlike all that I perceive through my senses. It transcends the senses. But it is possible to reason out the existence of God to a limited extent.

YI, 11 Oct. 1928

JANUARY 2

I do dimly perceive that whilst everything around me is ever-changing, ever-dying, there is underlying all that change a Living Power that is changeless, that holds all together, that creates, dissolves, and re-creates. That informing Power or Spirit is God. And since nothing else I see merely through the senses can or will persist, He alone is.

Ibid.

JANUARY 3

And is this Power benevolent or malevolent? I see it is purely benevolent. For I can see that in the midst of death life

3

persists, in the midst of untruth truth persists, in the midst of darkness light persists. Hence I gather that God is Life, Truth, Light. He is Love, He is the Supreme Good.
YI, 11 Oct. 1928

JANUARY 4

I cannot account for the existence of evil by any rational method. To want to do so is to be co-equal with God. I am, therefore, humble enough to recognize evil as such; and I call God long-suffering and patient precisely because He permits evil in the world.

Ibid.

JANUARY 5

I know that He has no evil in Him and yet if there is evil, He is the author of it and yet untouched by it. I know too that I shall never know God if I do not wrestle with and against evil even at the cost of life itself.

Ibid.

JANUARY 6

We do not know all the laws of God nor their working. Knowledge of the tallest scientist or the greatest spiritualist is like a particle of dust. If God is not a personal being for me like my earthly father, He is infinitely more. He rules me in the tiniest detail of my life. I believe literally that not a leaf moves but by His will. Every breath I take depends upon His sufferance.

H, 16 Feb. 1934

JANUARY 7

He and His Law are one. The Law is God. Anything attributed to Him is not a mere attribute. He is the attribute. He is Truth, Love and Law and a million other things that human ingenuity can name.

Ibid.

JANUARY 8

Perfection is the attribute of the Almighty, and yet what a great democrat He is! What an amount of wrong and humbug He suffers on our part! He even suffers insignificant creatures of His to question His very existence, though He is in every atom about us, around us and within us. But, He has reserved to Himself the right of becoming manifest to whomsoever He chooses. He is a Being without hands and feet and other organs, yet He can see him to whom He chooses to reveal Himself.

H, 14 Nov. 1936

JANUARY 9

To me God is Truth and Love; God is ethics and morality; God is fearlessness. God is the source of Light and Life and yet He is above and beyond all these. God is conscience. He is even the atheism of the atheist. For in His boundless love God permits the atheist to live.

YI, 5 March 1925

JANUARY 10

He is the searcher of hearts. He transcends speech and reason. He knows us and our hearts better than we do ourselves. He does not take us at our word, for He knows that we often do not mean it, some knowingly and others unknowingly.

YI, 5 March 1925

JANUARY 11

He is a personal God to those who need His personal presence. He is embodied to those who need His touch. He is the purest essence. He simply is to those who have faith. He is all things to all men. He is in us and yet above and beyond us.

Ibid.

JANUARY 12

He cannot cease to be because hideous immoralities or inhuman brutalities are committed in His name. He is long-suffering. He is patient but He is also terrible. He is the most exacting personage in the world and the world to come. He metes out the same measure to us that we mete out to our neighbours — men and brutes. With Him ignorance is no excuse. And withal He is ever forgiving for He always gives us the chance to repent.

Ibid.

JANUARY 13

He is the greatest democrat the world knows, for He leaves us *unfettered* to make our own choice between evil and good. He is the greatest tyrant ever known, for He often dashes the cup from our lips and under the cover of free will leaves us a margin so wholly inadequate as to provide only mirth for Himself at our expense.

Therefore it is that Hinduism calls it all His sport — *lila*, or calls it all an illusion — *maya*.

YI, 5 March 1925

JANUARY 14

God is not outside this earthly case of ours. Therefore, exterior proof is not of much avail, if any at all. We must ever fail to perceive Him through the senses, because He is beyond them. We can feel Him, if we will but withdraw ourselves from the senses. The divine music is incessantly going on within ourselves, but the loud senses drown the delicate music, which is unlike and infinitely superior to anything we can perceive or hear with our senses.

H, 13 June 1936

JANUARY 15

God is the hardest taskmaster I have known on this earth, and He tries you through and through. And when you find that your faith is failing or your body is failing you, and you are sinking, He comes to your assistance somehow or other and proves to you that you must not lose your faith and that He is always at your beck and call, but on His terms, not on your terms. So I have found. I cannot really recall a single instance when, at the eleventh hour, He has forsaken me.

SW, p. 1069

JANUARY 16

The divine guidance often comes when the horizon is the blackest.

YI, 27 Aug. 1925

JANUARY 17

God helps when one feels onself humbler than the very dust under one's feet. Only to the weak and helpless is divine succour vouchsafed.

SSA, p. 6

JANUARY 18

Mankind is notoriously too dense to read the signs that God sends from time to time. We require drums to be beaten into our ears, before we would wake from our trance and hear the warning and see that to lose oneself in all is the only way to find oneself.

YI, 25 Aug. 1927

9

JANUARY 19

If you would ask Him to help you, you would go to Him in all your nakedness, approach Him without reservations, also without fear or doubts as to how He can help a fallen being like you. He who has helped millions who have approached Him, is He going to desert you?

YI, 1 March 1929

JANUARY 20

Man's ultimate aim is the realization of God, and all his activities, social, political, religious, have to be guided by the ultimate aim of the vision of God. The immediate service of all human beings becomes a necessary part of the endeavour, simply because the only way to find God is to see Him in His creation and be one with it. This can only be done by service of all. I am a part and parcel of the whole, and I cannot find Him apart from the rest of humanity.

H, 29 Aug. 1936

JANUARY 21

God is a very hard taskmaster. He is never satisfied with fireworks display. His mills although they grind surely and incessantly grind excruciatingly slow and He is never satisfied with hasty forfeitures of life. It is a sacrifice of the purest that He demands, and so you and I have prayerfully to plod on, live out the life so long as it is vouchsafed to us to live it.

YI, 22 Sept. 1927

JANUARY 22

God keeps an accurate record of all things good and bad. There is no better accountant on earth.

H, 21 Sept. 1934

JANUARY 23

If God was a capricious person instead of being the changeless, unchangeable living law, He would in sheer indignation wipe out those who in the name of religion deny Him and His Law.

YI, 11 July 1929

JANUARY 24

God tries His votaries through and through, but never beyond endurance. He gives them strength enough to go through the ordeal He prescribes for them.

YI, 19 Feb. 1925

JANUARY 25

God to be God must rule the heart and transform it. He must express Himself in every smallest act of His votary. This can only be done through a definite realization more real than the five senses can ever produce.

YI, 11 Oct. 1928

JANUARY 26

Where there is realization outside the senses it is infallible. It is proved not by extraneous evidence but in the transformed conduct and character of those who have felt the real presence of God within. Such testimony is to be found in the experiences of an unbroken line of prophets and sages in all countries and climes. To reject this evidence is to deny oneself.

Ibid.

JANUARY 27

But it is impossible for us to realize perfect Truth so long as we are imprisoned in this mortal frame. We can only visualize it in our imagination. We cannot, through the instrumentality of this ephemeral body, see face to face Truth which is eternal. That is why in the last resort we must depend on faith.

YM, Chap. II

JANUARY 28

No one can attain perfection while he is in the body for the simple reason that the ideal state is impossible so long as one has not completely overcome his ego, and ego cannot be wholly got rid of so long as one is tied down by the shackles of the flesh.

YI, 20 Sept. 1928

JANUARY 29

Our existence as embodied beings is purely momentary; what are a hundred years in eternity? But if we shatter the chains of egotism, and melt into the ocean of humanity, we share its dignity. To feel that we are something is to set up a barrier between God and ourselves; to cease feeling that we are something is to become one with God.

YM, Chap. XII

JANUARY 30

A drop in the ocean partakes of the greatness of its parent, although it is un-

conscious of it. But it is dried up as soon
as it enters upon an existence independent
of the ocean. We do not exaggerate when
we say that life is a bubble.

YM, Chap. II

JANUARY 31

As soon as we become one with the
ocean in the shape of God, there is no more
rest for us, nor indeed do we need rest any
longer. Our very sleep is action. For we
sleep with the thought of God in our hearts.
This restlessness constitutes true rest. This
never-ceasing agitation holds the key to
peace ineffable. This supreme state of total
surrender is difficult to describe, but not
beyond the bounds of human experience.
It has been attained by many dedicated
souls, and may be attained by ourselves
as well.

Ibid.

FEBRUARY 1

Where Love is, there God is also.
SSA, p. 360

FEBRUARY 2

Love never claims, it ever gives. Love ever suffers, never resents, never revenges itself.

YI, 9 July 1925

FEBRUARY 3

I believe that the sum total of the energy of mankind is not to bring us down but to lift us up, and that is the result of the definite, if unconscious, working of the law of love. The fact that mankind persists shows that the cohesive force is greater than the disruptive force, centripetal force greater than centrifugal.

YI, 12 Nov. 1931

FEBRUARY 4

Scientists tell us that without the presence of the cohesive force amongst the atoms that comprise this globe of ours, it would crumble to pieces and we would cease to exist; and even as there is cohesive force in blind matter, so must there be in all things animate and the name for that cohesive force among animate beings is Love.

YI, 5 May 1920

FEBRUARY 5

We notice it between father and son, between brother and sister, friend and friend. But we have to learn to use that force among all that lives, and in the use of it consists our knowledge of God. Where there is love there is life; hatred leads to destruction.

Ibid.

FEBRUARY 6

I have found that life persists in the midst of destruction and therefore there must be a higher law than that of destruction. Only under that law would a well-ordered society be intelligible and life worth living.

YI, 1 Oct. 1931

FEBRUARY 7

If love was not the law of life, life would not have persisted in the midst of death. Life is a perpetual triumph over the grave.

H, 26 Sept. 1936

FEBRUARY 8

If there is a fundamental distinction between man and beast, it is the former's progressive recognition of the law and its application in practice to his own personal life. All the saints of the world, ancient and modern, were each according to his light and capacity a living illustration of that supreme Law of our Being.

Ibid.

FEBRUARY 9

The forms are many, but the informing spirit is one. How can there be room for distinctions of high and low where there is this all-embracing fundamental unity underlying the outward diversity? For that is a fact meeting you at every step in daily life. The final goal of all religions is to realize this essential oneness.

H, 15 Dec. 1933

FEBRUARY 10

We must widen the circle of our love till it embraces the whole village; the village in its turn must take into its fold the district, the district the province, and so on till the scope of our love becomes coterminous with the world.

YI, 27 June 1929

FEBRUARY 11

Not killing competition, but life-giving co-operation, is the law of the human being. Ignoring the emotion is to forget that man has feelings. Not the good of the few, not even good of the many, but it is the good of all that we are made to promote, if we are 'made in His own image'.

SW, p. 350

FEBRUARY 12

The golden rule of conduct . . . is mutual toleration, seeing that we will never all think alike and we shall always see Truth in fragment and from different angles of vision.

YI, 23 Sept. 1926

FEBRUARY 13

A seeker after Truth, a follower of the Law of Love, cannot hold anything against tomorrow. God never provides for the morrow. He never creates more than what is strictly needed from day to day. If, therefore, we repose faith in His Providence, we should rest assured that He will give us every day our daily bread, supplying enough that we require.

YI, 4 Sept. 1930

18

FEBRUARY 14

We are either ignorant or negligent of the Divine Law in virtue of which man has been given only his daily bread and no more, with the result that there arise inequalities with all the misery attendant upon them.

Ibid.

FEBRUARY 15

The rich have a superfluous store of things which they do not need and which are, therefore, neglected and wasted; while millions starve and are frozen to death for want of them. If each retained possession only of what he needed, none would be in want and all would live in contentment.

Ibid.

FEBRUARY 16

As it is, the rich are discontented no less than the poor. The poor man would become a millionaire and the millionaire a multimillionaire. The poor are often not satisfied when they get just enough to fill their stomachs; but they are clearly entitled to it and society should make it a point to see that they get it.

Ibid.

FEBRUARY 17

Our civilization, our culture, our Swaraj depend not upon multiplying our wants—self-indulgence, but upon restricting our wants—self-denial.

YI, 6 Oct. 1921

FEBRUARY 18

We should be ashamed of resting, or having a square meal so long as there is one able-bodied man or woman without work or food.

YI, 5 Feb. 1925

FEBRUARY 19

I suggest we are thieves in a way. If I take anything that I do not need for my own immediate use and keep it, I thieve it from somebody else.

SW, p. 384

FEBRUARY 20

I venture to suggest that it is the fundamental law of Nature, without exception, that Nature produces enough for our wants from day to day, and if only everybody took enough for himself and nothing more, there would be no pauperism in this world, there would be no man dying of starvation in this world.

Ibid.

FEBRUARY 21

I am no socialist and I do not want to dispossess those who have got possessions: but I do say that personally those of us who want to see light out of darkness have to follow this rule. I do not want to dispossess anybody. I should then be departing from the rule of *Ahimsa*. If somebody else possesses more than I do, let him. But so far as my own life has to be regulated, I dare not possess anything which I do not want.

Ibid.

FEBRUARY 22

In India we have got three millions of people who have to be satisfied with one meal a day, and that meal consisting of a *chapati* containing no fat in it and a pinch of salt. You and I have no right to anything that we really have until these three millions are clothed and fed better. You and I, who ought to know better, must adjust our wants, and even undergo voluntary starvation in order that they may be nursed, fed and clothed.

SW, p. 385

FEBRUARY 23

The golden rule . . . is resolutely to refuse to have what millions cannot. This ability to refuse will not descend upon us all of a sudden. The first thing is to cultivate the mental attitude that will not have possession or facilities denied to millions, and the next immediate thing is to re-arrange our lives as fast as possible in accordance with that mentality.

YI, 24 June 1926

FEBRUARY 24

One should eat not in order to please the palate, but just to keep body going. When each organ of sense subserves the body and through the body the soul, its special relish disappears and then alone does it begin to function in the way nature intended it to do. Any number of experiments is too small and no sacrifice too great for attaining this symphony with nature.

Auto, p. 392

FEBRUARY 25

We want healers of souls rather than
of bodies. The multiplicity of hospitals and
medical men is no sign of true civilization.
The less we and others pamper our bodies
the better for us and the world.

YI, 29 Sept. 1927

FEBRUARY 26

Instead of using the body as a temple
of God we use it as a vehicle for indulgences
and are not ashamed to run to medical
men for help in our effort to increase them
and abuse the earthly tabernacle.

YI, 8 Aug. 1929

FEBRUARY 27

Man's nature is not ·essentially evil.
Brute nature has been known to yield to
the influence of love. You must never
despair of human nature.

H, 5 Nov. 1938

FEBRUARY 28

Man's estate is one of probation. During that period he is played upon by evil
forces as well as good. He is ever prey to

temptations. He has to prove his manliness by resisting and fighting temptations.

H, 4 April 1936

FEBRUARY 29

It may be long before the law of love will be recognized in international affairs. The machineries of governments stand between and hide the hearts of one people from those of another.

YI, 23 June 1919

MARCH 1

Truth is like a vast tree, which yields more and more fruit, the more you nurture it. The deeper the search in the mine of Truth the richer the discovery of the gems buried there, in the shape of openings for an ever greater variety of service.

Auto, p. 218

MARCH 2

The seeker after Truth should be humbler than the dust. The world crushes the dust under its feet, but the seeker after Truth should so humble himself that even the

24

dust could crush him. Only then, and not until then, will he have a glimpse of truth.

Ibid., p. XVI

March 3

Devotion to Truth is the sole reason for our existence. All our activities should be centred in Truth. Truth should be the very breath of our life. When once this stage in the pilgrim's progress is reached, all other rules of correct living will come without effort, and obedience to them will be instinctive. But without Truth it would be impossible to observe any principles or rules in life.

YI, 30 July 1931

March 4

There should be Truth in thought, Truth in speech, and Truth in action. To the man who has realized this Truth in perfection, nothing else remains to be known, because all knowledge is necessarily included in it. What is not included in it is not Truth and so not true knowledge; and there can be no inward peace without the true knowledge. If we once learn how to apply this never-failing test of Truth,

25

we will at once be able to find out what
is worth being, what is worth seeing and
what is worth reading.

Ibid.

MARCH 5

The quest of Truth involves *tapas*—
self-suffering, sometimes even unto death.
There can be no place in it for even a trace
of self-interest. In such selfless search for
Truth nobody can lose his bearings for long.
Directly one takes to the wrong path one
stumbles and is thus redirected to the right
path. Therefore the pursuit of Truth is
true *bhakti* (devotion). It is the path that
leads to God and therefore there is no
place in it for cowardice, no place for
defeat. It is the talisman by which death
itself becomes the portal to life eternal.

YI, 30 July 1931

MARCH 6

It is not given to man to know the whole
Truth. His duty lies in living up to the
Truth as he sees it and in doing so to resort
to the purest means, i.e., to non-violence.

H, 24 Nov. 1933

MARCH 7

If observance of Truth was a bed of roses, if Truth cost one nothing and was all happiness and ease, there would be no beauty about it. We must adhere to Truth even if the heavens should fall.

YI, 27 Sept. 1928

MARCH 8

Only Truth quenches untruth, Love quenches anger, self-suffering quenches violence. This eternal rule is a rule not for saints only but for all. Those who observe it may be few but they are the salt of the earth, it is they who keep the society together, not those who sin against light and truth.

H, 1 Feb. 1942

MARCH 9

Abstract Truth has no value, unless it incarnates in human beings who represent it by proving their readiness to die for it. Our wrongs live because we only pretend to be their living representatives. The only way we can prove our claim is by readiness to suffer in the discharge of our trust.

YI, 22 Dec. 1921

MARCH 10

A man of Truth must ever be confident, if he has also equal need to be diffident. His devotion to Truth demands the fullest confidence. His consciousness of the human nature must make him humble and therefore ever ready to retrace his steps immediately he discovers his error.

YI, 6 May 1926

MARCH 11

Finite human beings shall never know in its fullness Truth and Love which is in itself infinite. But we do know enough for our guidance. We shall err, and sometimes grievously, in our application. But man is a self-governing being, and self-government necessarily includes the power as much to commit errors as to set them right as often as they are made.

YI, 21 April 1927

MARCH 12

I believe that if in spite of the best of intentions one is led into committing mistakes they do not really result in harm to the world or for the matter of that any individual. God always saves the world from

28

the consequences of unintended errors of men who live in fear of Him.

YI, 3 Jan. 1929

MARCH 13

To err, even grievously, is human. But it is human only if there is determination to mend the error and not to repeat it. The error will be forgotten if the promise is fully redeemed.

H, 6 Feb. 1937

MARCH 14

No niggardly acceptance of the inevitable will appear pleasing to God. It must be a thorough change of heart.

YI, 2 Feb. 1922

MARCH 15

There is no one without faults, not even men of God. They are men of God not because they are faultless but because they know their own faults, they strive against them, they do not hide them and are ever ready to correct themselves.

H, 28 Jan. 1939

MARCH 16

Confession of error is like a broom that sweeps away dirt and leaves the surface cleaner than before.

YI, 16 Feb. 1922

MARCH 17

Truth is not truth merely because it is ancient. Nor is it necessarily to be regarded with suspicion, because it is ancient. There are some fundamentals of life which may not be lightly given up because they are difficult of enforcement in one's life.

H, 14 March 1936

MARCH 18

Rationalists are admirable beings, rationalism is a hideous monster when it claims for itself omnipotence. Attribution of omnipotence to reason is as bad a piece of idolatry as is worship of stock and stone believing it to be God.

YI, 14 Oct. 1926

MARCH 19

Change is a condition of progress. An honest man cannot afford to observe mechanical consistency when the mind revolts against anything as an error.

YI, 19 Dec. 1929

MARCH 20

I make no hobgoblin of consistency. If I am true to myself from moment to moment, I do not mind all the inconsistencies that may be flung in my face.

H, 9 Nov. 1934

MARCH 21

There is a consistency that is wise and a consistency that is foolish. A man who in order to be consistent would go barebodied in the hot sun of India and sunless Norway in mid-winter would be considered a fool and would lose his life in the bargain.

YI, 4 April 1929

MARCH 22

Human life is a series of compromises and it is not always easy to achieve in practice what one has found to be true in theory.

H, 18 Nov. 1939

There are eternal principles which admit of no compromise and one must be prepared to lay down one's life in the practice of them.

H, 5 Sept. 1936

MARCH 24

In my opinion the Sanskrit text सत्यं ब्रूयात् प्रियं ब्रूयात् । न ब्रूयात् सत्यमप्रियम् ॥ (*Satyam bruyat priyam bruyat, Na bruyat satyamapriyam*) means that one should speak the truth in gentle language. One had better not speak it, if one cannot do so in a gentle way; meaning thereby that there is no truth in a man who cannot control his tongue.

YI, 17 Sept. 1925

MARCH 25

Nature has so made us that we do not see our backs; it is reserved for others to see them. Hence it is wise to profit by what they see.

DD, p. 224

MARCH 26

The pursuit of Truth is true *bhakti* (devotion). It is the path that leads to God, and, therefore, there is no place in it for cowardice, no place for defeat. It is the talisman by which death itself becomes the portal to the life eternal.

YM, Chap. I

March 27

From the standpoint of pure Truth, the body too is a possession. It has been truly said, that desire for enjoyment creates bodies for the soul. When this desire vanishes, there remains no further need for the body, and man is free from the vicious circle of births and deaths.

YM, Chap. VI

March 28

How beautiful it would be, if all of us, men and women, devoted ourselves wholly to Truth in all that we might do in our waking hours, whether working, eating, drinking, or playing, till dissolution of the body makes us one with Truth?

YM, Chap. I

March 29

Where there is no Truth, there can be no true knowledge. That is why the word

Chit or knowledge is associated with the name of God. And where there is true knowledge, there is always bliss (*Ananda*). Sorrow has no place there. And even as Truth is eternal, so is bliss derived from it. Hence we know God as *Sat-chit-ananda*, one who combines in Himself Truth, Knowledge and Bliss.

YM, 30 July 1931

MARCH 30

Silence is a great help to a seeker after truth. In the attitude of silence the soul finds the path in a clearer light and what is elusive and deceptive resolves itself into crystal clearness. Our life is a long and arduous quest after Truth, and the soul requires inward restfulness to attain its full height.

H, 10 Dec. 1938

MARCH 31

Experience has taught me that silence is a part of the spiritual discipline of a votary of truth. Proneness to exaggerate, to suppress or modify the truth wittingly or unwittingly, is a natural weakness of man, and silence is necessary in order to surmount it.

A man of few words will rarely be thoughtless in his speech; he will measure every word.

Auto, p. 62

APRIL 1

Religions are different roads converging upon the same point. What does it matter that we take different roads so long as we reach the same goal?

HS, p. 65

APRIL 2

Belief in one God is the corner-stone of all religions. But I do not foresee a time when there would be only one religion on earth in practice. In theory, since there is one God, there can be only one religion. But in practice, no two persons I have known have had the same identical conception of God. Therefore, there will perhaps always be different religions answering to different temperaments and climatic conditions.

H, 2 Feb. 1934

APRIL 3

I believe in the fundamental truth of all great religions of the world. I believe

that they are all God-given and I believe
that they were necessary for the people to
whom these religions were revealed. And
I believe that if only we could all of us
read the scriptures of the different faiths
from the standpoint of the followers of
these faiths, we should find that they were
at the bottom all one and were all helpful
to one another.

H, 16 Feb. 1934

APRIL 4

I believe that all the great religions of
the world are true more or less. I say 'more
or less' because I believe that everything
that the human hand touches by reason
of the very fact that human beings are
imperfect becomes imperfect.

YI, 22 Sept. 1927

APRIL 5

Perfection is the exclusive attribute
of God and it is undescribable, untransla-
table. I do believe that it is possible for
every human being to become perfect even
as God is perfect. It is necessary for all of
us to aspire after perfection, but when that

36

blessed state is attained, it becomes indescribable, indefinable.

YI, 22 Sept. 1927

APRIL 6

If we had attained the full vision of Truth, we would no longer be mere seekers, but would have become one with God, for Truth is God. But being only seekers we prosecute our quest and are conscious of our imperfection. And if we are imperfect ourselves, religion as conceived by us must also be imperfect.

YM, Chap. X

APRIL 7

We have not realized religion in its perfection, even as we have not realized God. Religion of our conception, being thus imperfect, is always subject to a process of evolution and re-interpretation. Progress towards Truth, towards God, is possible only because of such evolution. And if all faiths outlined by men are imperfect, the question of comparative merit does not arise.

YM, Chap. X

APRIL 8

All faiths constitute a revelation of Truth but all are imperfect, and liable to error. Reverence for other faiths need not blind us to their faults. We must be keenly alive to the defects of our own faith also, yet not leave it on that account, but try to overcome those defects. Looking at all religions with an equal eye, we would not only not hesitate, but would think it our duty, to blend into our faith every acceptable feature of other faiths.

Ibid.

APRIL 9

Even as a tree has a single trunk but many branches and leaves, so there is one true and perfect religion but it becomes many, as it passes through the human medium.

YM, Chap. X

APRIL 10

I came to the conclusion long ago, after prayerful search and study and discussion with as many people as I could meet, that all religions were true and also that all had some error in them, and that whilst I hold by my own, I should hold others as dear as Hinduism, from which it logically follows that we should hold all as dear as our nearest kith and kin and that we should make no distinction between them.

YI, 19 Jan. 1928

APRIL 11

The one religion is beyond all speech. Imperfect men put it into such language as they can command, and their words are interpreted by other men equally imperfect. Whose interpretation is to be held to be the right one? Everybody is right from his own standpoint, but it is not impossible that everybody is wrong. Hence the necessity of tolerance, which does not mean indifference to one's own faith, but a more intelligent and purer love for it.

YM, Chap. X

APRIL 12

Tolerance gives us spiritual insight, which is as far from fanaticism as the north pole from the south. True knowledge of religion breaks down the barriers between faith and faith.

Ibid.

April 13

It is not necessary for toleration that I must approve of what I tolerate. I heartily dislike drinking, meat-eating and smoking, but I tolerate these in Hindus, Mahomedans and Christians, even as I expect them to tolerate my abstinence from all these, although they may dislike it.

YI, 25 Feb. 1920

April 14

Religion which takes no account of practical affairs and does not help to solve them is no religion.

YI, 7 May 1925

April 15

I do not know any religion apart from human activity. It provides a moral basis to all other activities which they would otherwise lack, reducing life to a maze of 'sound and fury signifying nothing'.

H, 24 Dec. 1938

April 16

For me, politics bereft of religion is absolute dirt ever to be shunned. Politics concern nations and that which concerns the welfare of nations must be one of the concerns of a man who is religiously inclined, in other words a seeker after God and Truth.

YI, 18 June 1925

APRIL 17

For me, God and Truth are convertible terms and if anyone told me that God was a god of untruth or a god of torture I would decline to worship him. Therefore, in politics also we have to establish the Kingdom of Heaven.

YI, 18 June 1925

APRIL 18

A good Hindu or a good Musalman should be a better Hindu or a better Musalman for being a lover of his country. There never can be any conflict between the real interest of one's country and that of one's religion. Where there appears to be any there is something wrong with one's religion, i.e., one's morals. True religion means good thought and good conduct. True patriotism also means good thought and good conduct. To set up a comparison between two synonymous things is wrong.

YI, 9 Jan. 1930

41

APRIL 19

We the human family are not all philosophers. We are of the earth very earthy, and we are not satisfied with contemplating the Invisible God. Somehow or other we want something which we can touch, something which we can see, something before which we can kneel down. It does not matter whether it is a book, or an empty stone building or a stone building inhabited by numerous figures. A book will satisfy some, an empty building will satisfy some others, and many others will not be satisfied unless they see something inhabiting these empty buildings.

H, 23 Jan. 1937

APRIL 20

It depends on our mental condition whether we gain something or do not gain something by going to the temples. We have to approach these temples in a humble and penitent mood. They are so many homes of God. Of course God resides in every human form, indeed every particle of His creation, everything that is on this earth. But since we very fallible mortals do not appreciate the fact that God is every-

42

where we impute special sanctity to temples and think that God resides there.

H, 23 Jan. 1937

APRIL 21

When we approach these temples we must cleanse our bodies, our minds and our hearts and we should enter them in a prayerful mood and ask God to make us purer men and purer women for having entered their portals. And if you will take this advice of an old man, this physical deliverance that you have secured will be a deliverance of the soul.

Ibid.

APRIL 22

Bitter experience has taught me that all temples are not houses of God. They can be habitations of the devil. These places of worship have no value unless the keeper is a good man of God. Temples, mosques, churches are what man makes them to be.

YI, 19 May 1927

APRIL 23

If anyone doubts the infinite mercy of God, let him have a look at these sacred places. How much hypocrisy and irreligion does the prince of Yogis suffer to be perpetrated in His holy name?

Auto, p. 242

APRIL 24

Churches, mosques and temples which cover so much hypocrisy and humbug and shut the poorest out of them seem but a mockery of God and His worship when one sees the eternally renewed temple of worship under the vast blue canopy inviting every one of us to real worship, instead of abusing His name by quarrelling in the name of religion.

H, 5 March 1942

APRIL 25

Untouchability poisons Hinduism as a drop of arsenic poisons milk.

YI, 20 Dec. 1927

APRIL 26

The 'touch-me-not'ism that disfigures the present-day Hinduism is a morbid growth. It only betrays a woodenness of mind, a blind self-conceit. It is abhorrent alike to the spirit of religion and morality.

H, 20 April 1934

April 27

It is to my mind a curse that has come to us and as long as that curse remains with us, so long I think we are bound to consider that every affliction that we labour under in this sacred land is a fit and proper punishment for this great and indelible crime that we are committing.

SW, p. 387

April 28

Shall we have not the vision to see that in suppressing a sixth (or whatever the number) of ourselves, we have depressed ourselves? No man takes another down a pit without descending into it himself and sinning in the bargain. It is not the suppressed that sin. It is the suppressor who has to answer for his crime against those whom he suppresses.

YI, 29 March 1928

April 29

God does not punish directly. His ways are inscrutable. Who knows that all our woes are not due to that one black sin?

YI, 29 March 1924

APRIL 30

Swaraj is a meaningless term, if we desire to keep a fifth of India under perpetual subjection, and deliberately deny to them the fruits of national culture. We are seeking the aid of God in this great purifying movement, but we deny to the most deserving among His creatures the rights of humanity. Inhuman ourselves, we may not plead before the throne for deliverance from the inhumanity of others.

YI, 25 May 1921

MAY 1

Prayer is the key of the morning and the bolt of the evening.

YI, 23 Jan. 1930

MAY 2

As food is necessary for the body, prayer is necessary for the soul. A man may be able to do without food, for a number of days—as MacSwiney did for over seventy days—but, believing in God, man cannot, should not, live a moment ·without prayer.

YI, 15 Dec. 1927

MAY 3

Prayer needs no speech. It is in itself independent of any sensuous effort. I have not the slightest doubt that prayer is an unfailing means of cleansing the heart of passion. But it must be combined with the utmost humility.

Auto, p. 72

MAY 4

I am giving you a bit of my experience and that of my companions when I say that he who has experienced the magic of prayer may do without food for days together but not a single moment without prayer. For without prayer there is no inward peace.

YI, 23 Jan. 1930

MAY 5

Never own defeat in a sacred cause and make up your minds henceforth that you will be pure and that you will find a response from God. But God never answers the prayers of the arrogant, nor the prayers of those who bargain with Him.

YI, 4 April 1929

47

MAY 6

I can give my own testimony and say that a heartfelt prayer is undoubtedly the most potent instrument that man possesses for overcoming cowardice and all other bad old habits. Prayer is an impossibility without a living faith in the presence of God within.

YI, 20 Dec. 1928

MAY 7

The prayer of even the most impure will be answered. I am telling this out of my personal experience, I have gone through the purgatory. Seek first the Kingdom of Heaven and everything will be added unto you.

YI, 4 April 1929

MAY 8

Not until we have reduced ourselves to nothingness can we conquer the evil in us. God demands nothing less than complete self-surrender as the price for the only real freedom that is worth having. And when a man thus loses himself he immediately finds himself in the service of all that lives. It becomes his delight and his recreation. He is a new man, never weary of spending himself in the service of God's creation.

YI, 20 Dec. 1928

MAY 9

Our prayer is a heart search. It is a reminder to ourselves that we are helpless without His support. No effort is complete without prayer—without a definite recognition that the best human endeavour is of no effect if it has not God's blessing ·behind. Prayer is a call to humility. It is a call to self-purification, to inward search.

H, 8 June 1935

MAY 10

There are limits to the capacity of an individual and the moment he flatters himself that he can undertake all tasks, God is there to humble his pride.

YI, 12 March 1931

MAY 11

Man is a fallible being. He can never be sure of his steps. What he may regard as answer to prayer may be an echo of his

pride. For infallible guidance man has to
have a perfectly innocent heart incapable
of evil.

YI, 25 Sept. 1931

MAY 12

Let everyone try and find that as a
result of daily prayer he adds something
new to his life, something with which nothing
can be compared.

YI, 24 Sept. 1924

MAY 13

There are subjects where reason cannot
take us far and we have to accept things
on faith. Faith then does not contradict
reason but transcends it. Faith is a kind
of sixth sense which works in cases which
are without the purview of reason.

H, 6 March 1937

MAY 14

Without faith this world would come
to naught in a moment. True faith is
appropriation of the reasoned experience of
people whom we believe to have lived a life
purified by prayer and penance. Belief

therefore in prophets or incarnations who have lived in remote ages is not an idle superstition but a satisfaction of an inmost spiritual want.

YI, 14 April 1927

MAY 15

A man without faith is like a drop thrown out of the ocean bound to perish. Every drop in the ocean shares its majesty and has the honour of giving us the ozone of life.

H, 25 April 1936

MAY 16

Faith is a function of the heart. It must be enforced by reason. The two are not antagonistic as some think. The more intense one's faith is, the more it whets one's reason. When faith becomes blind it dies.

H, 6 April 1940

MAY 17

It is faith that steers us through stormy seas, faith that moves mountains and faith that jumps across the oceans. That faith is nothing but a living, wide-awake consciousness of god within. He who has achieved that faith wants nothing. Bodily diseased, he is spiritually healthy, physically poor, he rolls in spiritual riches.

YI, 24 Sept. 1925

MAY 18

I am a man of faith. My reliance is solely on God. One step is enough for me. The next step he will make clear to me when time for it comes.

H, 20 Oct. 1940

MAY 19

That faith is of little value which can flourish only in fair weather. Faith in order to be of any value has to survive the severest trials. Your faith is a whited sepulchre if it cannot stand the calumny of the whole world.

YI, 25 April 1929

MAY 20

Faith is not a delicate flower which would wither under the slightest stormy weather. Faith is like the Himalaya mountains which cannot possibly change. No storm can possibly remove the Himalaya mountains from their foundation. . . . And I want every one of you to cultivate that faith in God and religion.

H, 26 Jan. 1934

MAY 21

If we have faith in us, if we have a prayerful heart, we may not tempt God, may not make terms with Him. We must reduce ourselves to a cipher.

YI, 22 Dec. 1928

MAY 22

There is a divine purpose behind every physical calamity. That perfected science will one day be able to tell us beforehand when earthquakes will occur, as it tells us today of eclipses, is quite possible. It will be another triumph of the human mind. But such triumphs even indefinitely multiplied can bring about no purification of self without which nothing is of any value.

H, 8 June 1935

MAY 23

This earthly existence of ours is more brittle than the glass bangles that ladies wear. You can keep glass bangles for thousands of years if you treasure them in a chest and let them remain untouched. But this earthly existence is so fickle that it may be wiped out in the twinkling of an eye. Therefore while we get breathing time, let us get rid of the distinctions of high and low, purify our hearts and be ready to face our maker when an earthquake or some natural calamity or death in the ordinary course overtakes us.

H, 2 Feb. 1934

MAY 24

Death, which is an eternal verity, is revolution, as birth and after is slow and steady evolution. Death is as necessary for a man's growth as life itself.

YI, 2 Feb. 1922

MAY 25

Death is no friend, he is the truest of friends. He delivers us from agony. He helps us against ourselves. He ever gives us new chances, new hopes. He is like sleep a sweet restorer.

YI, 20 Dec. 1926

MAY 26

It is as clear to me as daylight that life and death are but phases of the same thing, the reverse and obverse of the same coin. In fact tribulation and death seem to me to present a phase far richer than happiness of life. What is life worth without trials and tribulation which are the salt of life?

YI, 12 March 1930

MAY 27

My religion teaches me that whenever there is distress which one cannot remove, one must fast and pray.

YI, 25 Sept. 1924

MAY 28

There is nothing so powerful as fasting and prayer that would give us the requisite discipline, spirit of self-sacrifice, humility and resoluteness of will without which there can be no real progress.

YI, 31 March 1920

MAY 29

Fasting is a potent weapon in the Satyagraha armoury. It cannot be taken by everyone. Mere physical capacity to take it is no qualification for it. It is of no use without a living faith in God. It should never be a mechanical effort nor a mere imitation. It must come from the depth of one's soul.

H, 18 March 1939

MAY 30

One fasts for health's sake under laws governing health, fasts as a penance for a wrong done and felt as such. In these fasts, the fasting one need not believe in *ahimsa*. There is, however, a fast which every votary of non-violence sometimes feels impelled to undertake by way of protest against some wrong done by society and this he does when he as a votary of *ahimsa* has no other remedy left.

DD, p. 330

MAY 31

A complete fast is a complete and literal denial of self. It is the truest prayer. 'Take my life and let it be always, only, all for Thee' is not, should not be, a mere lip or figurative expression. It has to be a reckless and joyous giving without the least reservation. Abstention from food and even water is but the mere beginning, the least part of the surrender.

H, 13 April 1933

June 1

If we realized the presence of God as witness to all we say and do we would not have anything to conceal from anybody on earth. For we would not think unclean thoughts before our Maker, much less speak them. It is uncleanness that seeks secrecy and darkness.

YI, 22 Dec. 1920

June 2

The tendency of human nature is to hide dirt, we do not want to see or touch dirty things; we want to put them out of sight. And so must it be with our speech. I would suggest that we should avoid even thinking thoughts we would hide from the world.

Ibid.

June 3

Whatever you do, be true to yourselves and to the world. Hide not your thoughts.

If it is shameful to reveal them, it is more shameful to think them.

H, 24 April 1937

JUNE 4

All sins are committed in secrecy. The moment we realize that God witnesses even our thoughts we shall be free.

H, 17 Jan. 1939

JUNE 5

Control over thought is a long and painful and laborious process. But I am convinced that no time, no labour and no pain is too much for the glorious result to be reached. The purity of thought is possible only with a faith in God bordering on definite experience.

YI, 25 Aug. 1927

JUNE 6

When your passions threaten to get the better of you, go down on your knees and cry out to God for help. *Ramanama* is my infallible Help.

SRSI, Part II, p. ix

June 7

Let every aspirant after a pure life take from me that an impure thought is often powerful in undermining the body as an impure act.

YI, 25 Aug. 1927

June 8

The potency of thought unsuppressed but unembodied is far greater than that of thought embodied that is translated into action. And when the action is brought under due control, it reacts upon and regulates the thought itself. Thought thus translated into action becomes a prisoner and is brought under subjection.

YI, 2 Sept. 1926

June 9

Always aim at complete harmony of thought and word and deed. Always aim at purifying your thoughts and everything will be well. There is nothing more potent than thought. Deed follows word and word follows thought. The world is the result of a mighty thought and where the thought is mighty and pure the result is always mighty and pure.

H, 24 April 1937

JUNE 10

Man often becomes what he believes himself to be. If I keep on saying to myself that I cannot do a certain thing, it is possible that I may end by really becoming incapable of doing it. On the contrary, if I have the belief that I can do it, I shall surely acquire the capacity to do it even if I may not have it at the beginning.

H, 1 Sept. 1940

JUNE 11

Prayerful well-meaning effort never goes in vain and man's success lies only in such an effort. The result is in his hands.

YI, 17 June 1931

JUNE 12

'Be thou certain, none can perish, trusting Me,' says the Lord, but let it not be understood to mean that our sins will be washed away by merely trusting Him without any striving. Only he who struggles hard against the allurements of sense objects and turns in tears and grief to the Lord will be comforted.

YI, 12 Jan. 1928

JUNE 13

It is easy enough to say, 'I do not believe in God.' For God permits all things to be said of Him with impunity. He looks at our acts. And any breach of His Law carries with it, not its vindictive, but its purifying, compelling, punishment.

YI, 23 Sept. 1926

JUNE 14

The path of self-purification is hard and steep. To attain to perfect purity one has to become absolutely passion-free in thought, speech and action; to rise above the opposing currents of love and hatred, attachment and repulsion.

Auto, p. 504

JUNE 15

I believe that a healthy soul should inhabit a healthy body. To the extent, therefore, that the soul grows into health and freedom from passion, to that extent the body also grows into that state.

YI, 5 June 1924

June 16

Cleanliness is next to godliness. We can no more gain God's blessings with an unclean body than with an unclean mind. A clean body cannot reside in an unclean city.

YI, 19 Nov. 1925

June 17

Restraint never ruins one's health. What ruins one's health is not restraint but outward suppression. A really self-restrained person grows every day from strength to strength and from peace to more peace. The very first step in self-restraint is the restraint of thoughts.

H, 28 Oct. 1937

June 18

An innocent youth is a priceless possession not to be squandered away for the sake of a momentary excitement, miscalled pleasure.

H, 21 Sept. 1935

June 19

Steam becomes a mighty power only when it allows itself to be imprisoned in a strong little reservoir and produces tremendous motion and carries huge weights by permitting itself a tiny and measured outlet. Even so have the youth of the country of their own free will to allow their inexhaustible energy to be imprisoned, controlled and set free in strictly measured and required quantities.

YI, 30 Oct. 1929

JUNE 20

As a splendid palace deserted by its inmates looks like a ruin, so does a man without character, all his material belongings notwithstanding.

SSA, p. 355

JUNE 21

All our learning or recitation of the Vedas, correct knowledge of Sanskrit, Latin, Greek and what not will avail us nothing if they do not enable us to cultivate absolute purity of heart. The end of all knowledge must be building up of character.

YI, 8 Sept. 1927

June 22

Knowledge without character is a power for evil only, as seen in the instances of so many 'talented thieves' and 'gentleman rascals' in the world.

YI, 21 Feb. 1929

June 23

Drugs and drink are the two arms of the devil with which he strikes his helpless victims into stupefaction and intoxication.

YI, 12 April 1926

June 24

When Satan comes disguised as a champion of liberty, civilization, culture and the like, he makes himself almost irresistible.

YI, 11 July 1929

June 25

I hold drink to be more damnable than thieving and perhaps even prostitution. Is it not often the parent of both?

YI, 23 Feb. 1922

June 26

People drink because of the conditions to which they are reduced. It is the factory labourers and others that drink. They are forlorn, uncared for and they take to drink. They are no more vicious by nature than teetotallers are saints by nature. The majority of people are controlled by their environment.

YI, 8 Sept. 1927

June 27

Nothing but ruin stares a nation in the face that is a prey to the drink habit. History records that empires have been destroyed through that habit.

YI, 4 April 1929

June 28

There is as much flaw in the argument that it is an interference with the right of the people as there would be in the argument that the laws prohibiting theft interfere with the right of thieving. A thief steals all earthly possessions, a drunkard steals his own and his neighbours' honour.

YI, 6 Jan. 1927

June 29

I have a horror of smoking as of wines. Smoking I consider to be a vice. It deadens one's conscience and is often worse than drink in that it acts imperceptibly. It is a habit which is difficult to get rid of when once it seizes hold of a person. It is an expensive vice. It fouls the breath, discolours teeth and sometimes even causes cancer. It is an unclean habit.

YI, 12 Jan. 1921

June 30

Smoking is in a way a greater curse than drink inasmuch as the victim does not realize its evil in time. It is not regarded as a sign of barbarism, it is even acclaimed by the civilized people. I can only say, let those who can, give it up and set the example.

YI, 4 Feb. 1926

July 1

Non-violence is the law of our species as violence is the law of the brute. The spirit lies dormant in the brute and he knows no law but that of physical might. The

66

dignity of man requires obedience to a
higher law—to the strength of the spirit.

YI, 11 Sept. 1920

JULY 2

Non-violence is an active force of the
highest order. It is soul force or the power
of Godhead within us. Imperfect man
cannot grasp the whole of that essence—
he would not be able to bear its full blaze,
but even an infinitesimal fraction of it, when
it becomes active within us, can work
wonders.

H, 12 Nov. 1938

JULY 3

The sun in the heavens fills the whole
universe with its life-giving warmth. But
if one went too near it, it would consume
him to ashes. Even so, it is with Godhead.
We become God-like to the extent we
realize non-violence; but we can never
become wholly God.

H, 12 Nov. 1938

JULY 4

Non-violence is like radium in its action.
An infinitesimal quantity of it embedded

in a malignant growth, acts continuously, silently and ceaselessly till it has transformed the whole mass of the diseased tissue into a healthy one. Similarly, even a little of true non-violence acts in a silent, subtle, unseen way and leavens the whole society.

H, 12 Nov. 1938

JULY 5

Non-violence is the greatest force at the disposal of mankind. It is mightier than the mightiest weapon of destruction devised by the ingenuity of man. Destruction is not the law of the humans. Man lives freely by his readiness to die, if need be, at the hands of his brother, never by killing him. Every murder or other injury, no matter for what cause, committed or inflicted on another is a crime against humanity.

H, 20 July 1925

JULY 6

My creed of non-violence is an extremely active force. It has no room for cowardice or even weakness. There is hope for a violent man to be some day non-violent, but there is none for a coward. I have, therefore, said more than once ... that if we do not know how to defend ourselves, our women and our places of worship by the force of sufferings, i.e., non-violence, we must, if we are men, be at least able to defend all these by fighting.

YI, 16 June 1927

JULY 7

My non-violence does admit of people who cannot or will not be non-violent holding and making effective use of arms. Let me repeat for the thousandth time that non-violence is of the strongest, not of the weak.

TI, 8 May 1941

JULY 8

No matter how weak a person is in body, if it is a shame to flee. He will stand his ground and die at his post. This would be non-violence and bravery. No matter how weak he is, he will use what strength he has in inflicting injury on his opponent, and die in the attempt. This is bravery, but not non-violence. If, when his duty is to face danger, he flees, it is cowardice. In the first case the man will have love or charity in him. In the second and third cases, there would be a dislike or distrust and fear.

H, 17 Aug. 1935

JULY 9

If the best minds of the world have not imbibed the spirit of non-violence, they would have to meet gangsterism in the orthodox way. But that would only show that we have not gone far beyond the law of the jungle, that we have not yet learnt to appreciate the heritage that God has given us, that, in spite of the teaching of Christianity which is 1900 years old and of Hinduism and Buddhism which are older, and even of Islam, we have not made much headway as human beings. But whilst I would understand the use of force by those who have not the spirit of non-violence in them I would have those who know non-violence to throw their whole weight in demonstrating that even gangsterism has to be met with non-violence.

H, 10 Dec. 1938

JULY 10

Fearlessness is the first requisite of spirituality. Cowards can never be moral.

YI, 13 Oct. 1921

July 11

Let us fear God and we shall cease to fear man.

SW, p. 330

July 12

Self-sacrifice of one innocent man is a million times more potent than the sacrifice of million men who die in the act of killing others. The willing sacrifice of the innocent is the most powerful retort to insolent tyranny that has yet been conceived by God or man.

YI, 12 Feb. 1925

July 13

With Satya combined with Ahimsa, you can bring the world to your feet. Satyagraha in its essence is nothing but the introduction of truth and gentleness in the political, i.e., the national life.

YI, 10 March 1920

July 14

A Satyagrahi bids good-bye to fear. He is, therefore, never afraid of trusting the opponent. Even if the opponent p'ays him

false twenty times, the Satyagrahi is ready
to trust him the twenty-first time, for an
implicit trust in human nature is the very
essence of his creed.

SSA, p. 246

JULY 15

A Satyagrahi is nothing if not instinc-
tively law-abiding and it is his law-abiding
nature which exacts from him implicit
obedience to the highest law, that is the
voice of conscience which overrides all
other laws.

SW, p. 465

JULY 16

Satyagraha is gentle, it never wounds.
It must not be the result of anger or malice.
It is never fussy, never impatient, never
vociferous. It is the direct opposite of compul-
sion. It was conceived as a complete
substitute for violence.

H, 15 April 1933

JULY 17

It is force that may be used by individuals as well as by communities. It may
be used as well in political as in domestic

affairs. Its universal applicability is a demonstration of its permanence and invincibility. It can be used alike by men, women and children. It is totally untrue to say that it is a force to be used only by the weak so long as they are not capable of meeting violence by violence.

YI, 3 Nov. 1927

July 18

This force is to violence and therefore to all tyranny, all injustice, what light is to darkness. In politics, its use is based upon the immutable maxim, that government of the people is possible only so long as they consent either consciously or unconsciously to be governed.

Ibid.

July 19

The hardest heart and the grossest ignorance must disappear before the rising sun of suffering without anger and without malice.

YI, 10 Feb. 1925

July 20

In every great cause it is not the number of fighters that counts but it is the quality

73

of which they are made that becomes the deciding factor. The greatest men of the world have always stood alone.

YI, 10 Oct. 1929

JULY 21

Take the great prophets, Zoroaster, Buddha, Jesus, Mohammed — they stood alone like many others whom I can name. But they had living faith in themselves and their God, and believing as they did that God was on their side, they never felt lonely.

Ibid.

JULY 22

You may recall the occasion when pursued by a numerous enemy, Abu Bakr, who was accompanying the prophet in his flight, trembled to think of their fate and said, 'Look at the number of enemies that is overtaking us. What shall we two do against these heavy odds?' Without a moment's reflection the prophet rebuked his faithful companion by saying, 'No, Abu Bakr, we are three for God is with us!' Or take the invincible faith of Vibhishan and Prahlad. I want you to have that same living faith in yourselves and God.

YI, 10 Oct. 1929

July 23

All life in the flesh exists by some Himsa. Hence the highest religion has been defined by a negative word Ahimsa. The world is bound in a chain of destruction. In other words Himsa is an inherent necessity for life in the body. That is why a votary of Ahimsa always prays for ultimate deliverance from the bondage of flesh.

YI, 2 Oct. 1928

July 24

I do believe that all God's creatures have the right to live as much as we have. Instead of prescribing the killing of the so-called injurious fellow creatures of ours as a duty, if men of knowledge had devoted their gift to discovering ways of dealing with them otherwise than by killing them, we would be living in a world befitting our status as men — animals endowed with reason and the power of choosing between good and evil, right and wrong, violence and non-violence, truth and untruth.

H, 9 Jan. 1937

July 25

We are living in the midst of death trying to grope our way to Truth. Perhaps

75

it is as well that we are beset with danger at every point in our life, for, in spite of our knowledge of the danger and of our precarious existence, our indifference to the source of all life is excelled only by our amazing arrogance.

YI, 7 July 1927

JULY 26

Both my intellect and heart refuse to believe that the so-called noxious life has been created for destruction by man. God is good and wise. A good and wise God cannot be so bad and so unwise as to create to no purpose. It is more conducive to reason to own our ignorance and assume that every form of life has a useful purpose which we must patiently strive to discover.

H, 9 Jan. 1937

JULY 27

I verily believe that man's habit of killing man on the slightest pretext has darkened his reason and he gives himself liberties with other life which he would shudder to take if he really believed that God was a God of Love and Mercy.

Ibid.

JULY 28

I abhor vivisection with my whole soul. I detest the unpardonable slaughter of innocent life in the name of science and of humanity so-called, and all the scientific discoveries stained with innocent blood I count as of no consequence.

YI, 17 Dec. 1925

JULY 29

Means and ends are convertible terms in my philosophy of life.

YI, 26 Dec. 1924

JULY 30

They say, 'means are after all means'. I would say, 'means are after all everything'. As the means so the end. Violent means will give violent Swaraj. That would be a menace to the world and to India herself. France obtained her freedom by violent means. She is still paying dearly for her violence.

YI, 17 July 1924

JULY 31

There is no wall of separation between means and end. Indeed, the Creator has given us control (and that too very limited) over means, none over the end. Realization of the goal is in exact proportion to that of the means. This is a proposition that admits of no exception.

YI, 17 July 1924

AUGUST 1

Economics that hurt the moral well-being of an individual or a nation are immoral and therefore sinful. Thus, the economics that permit one country to prey upon another are immoral. It is sinful to buy and use articles made by sweated labour.

YI, 13 Oct. 1921

AUGUST 2

The economics that disregard moral and sentimental considerations are like wax works that being life-like still lack the life of the living flesh. At every crucial moment these new-fangled economic laws have broken down in practice. And nations or individuals who accept them as guiding maxims must perish.

YI, 27 Oct. 1921

August 3

The extension of the law of non-violence in the domain of economics means nothing less than the introduction of moral values as a factor to be considered in regulating international commerce.

YI, 26 Dec. 1924

August 4

I wholeheartedly detest this mad desire to destroy distance and time, to increase animal appetites and go to the ends of the earth in search of their satisfaction. If modern civilization stands for all this, and I have understood it to do so, I call it Satanic.

YI, 17 March 1927

August 5

I am not aiming at destroying railways or hospitals, though I would certainly welcome their natural destruction. Neither railways nor hospitals are a test of a high and pure civilization. At best they are a necessary evil. Neither adds one inch to the moral stature of a nation.

YI, 26 Jan. 1921

August 6

Is the world any the better for quick instruments of locomotion? How do these instruments advance man's spiritual progress? Do they not in the last resort hamper it? And is there any limit to man's ambition? Once we were satisfied with travelling a few miles an hour; today we want to negotiate hundreds of miles an hour; one day we might desire to fly through space. What will be the result? Chaos.

YI, 21 Jan. 1926

August 7

It is my firm belief that Europe today represents not the spirit of God or Christianity but the spirit of Satan. And Satan's successes are the greatest when he appears with the name of God on his lips. Europe is today only nominally Christian. In reality it is worshipping Mammon.

YI, 8 Sept. 1920

August 8

'Brahma created His people with the duty of sacrifice laid upon them and said: "By this do you flourish. Let it be the fulfiller of all your desires." 'He who eats without performing this sacrifice, eats stolen bread,' thus says the Gita.

H, 29 June 1935

AUGUST 9

'Earn thy bread by the sweat of thy brow,' says the Bible. Sacrifices may be of many kinds. One of them may well be breadlabour. If all laboured for their bread and no more, then there would be enough food and enough leisure for all.

Ibid.

AUGUST 10

Then there would be no cry of over-population, no disease, and no such misery as we see around. Such labour will be the highest form of sacrifice. Men will no doubt do many other things, either through their bodies or through their minds, but all this will be labour of love, for the common good. There will then be no rich and no poor, none high and none low, no touchable and no untouchable.

Ibid.

AUGUST 11

Even if, without fulfilling the whole law of sacrifice, that is, the law of our being, we perform physical labour enough for our daily bread, we should go a long way towards the ideal. If we did so, our wants would be minimized, our food would be simple. We should then eat to live, not live to eat. Let anyone who doubts the accuracy of this proposition try to sweat for his bread; he will derive the greatest relish from the productions of his labour, improve his health and discover that many things he took were superfluities.

H, 29 June 1935

AUGUST 12

I cannot picture to myself a time when no man shall be richer than another. But I do picture to myself a time when the rich will spurn to enrich themselves at the expense of the poor and the poor will cease to envy the rich. Even in a most perfect world, we shall fail to avoid inequalities, but we can and must avoid strife and bitterness.

YI, 7 Oct. 1926

AUGUST 13

The dream I want to realize is not the spoliation of the property of private owners, but to restrict its enjoyment so as to avoid

all pauperism, consequent discontent and
the hideously ugly contrast that exists today
between the lives and surroundings of the
rich and the poor.

YI, 21 Nov. 1929

August 14

Dead machinery must not be pitted
against the millions of living machines
represented by the villagers scattered in the
seven hundred thousand villages of India.

H, 14 Sept. 1935

August 15

Machinery to be well used has to help
and ease human effort. The present use
of machinery tends more and more to con-
centrate wealth in the hands of a few in
total disregard of millions of men and
women whose bread is snatched by it out
of their mouths.

Ibid.

August 16

The supreme consideration is man.
The machine should not tend to make
atrophied the limbs of man.

YI, 13 Nov. 1924

AUGUST 17

What I object to is the craze for machinery, not machinery as such. The craze is for what they call labour-saving machinery. Men go on 'saving labour', till thousands are without work and thrown on the open streets to die of starvation.

Ibid.

AUGUST 18

But why not, it is asked, save the labour of millions, and give them more leisure for intellectual pursuits? Leisure is good and necessary up to a point only. God created man to eat his bread in the sweat of his brow, and I dread the prospect of our being able to produce all that we want, including our food-stuffs, out of a conjuror's hat.

H, 16 May 1936

AUGUST 19

I want to save time and labour, not for a fraction of mankind, but for all. I want the concentration of wealth, not in the hands of a few, but in the hands of all. Today machinery merely helps a few to ride on the backs of millions. The impetus behind it all is not the philanthropy to save labour,

but greed. It is against this constitution
of things that I am fighting with all my
might.

YI, 13 Nov. 1924

AUGUST 20

The movement of the spinning wheel
is an organized attempt to displace machinery from that state of exclusiveness and
exploitation and to place it in its proper
state. Under my scheme, therefore, men
in charge of machinery will think not of
themselves or even of the nation to which
they belong but of the whole human race.

YI, 17 Sept. 1925

AUGUST 21

I claim for the Charkha the honour of
being able to solve the problem of economic
distress in a most natural, simple, inexpen-
sive and businesslike manner. The Charkha,
therefore, is not only not useless . . . but
is a useful and indispensable article for
every home. It is the symbol of the nation's
prosperity and, therefore, freedom. It is a
symbol not of commercial war but of commercial peace.

YI, 8 Dec. 1921

AUGUST 22

It bears not a message of ill-will towards the nations of the earth but of good-will and self-help. It will not need the protection of a navy threatening a world's peace and exploiting its resources, but it needs the religious determination of millions to spin their yarn in their homes as today they cook their food in their own homes.

Ibid.

AUGUST 23

As I look at Russia where the apotheosis of industrialization has been reached, the life there does not appeal to me. To use the language of the Bible, 'What shall it avail a man if he gain the whole world and lose his soul?' In modern terms, it is beneath human dignity to lose one's individuality and become a mere cog in the machine. I want every individual to become a full-blooded, full-developed member of the society.

H, 28 Jan. 1939

AUGUST 24

What does communism mean in the last analysis? It means a classless society—

an ideal that is worth striving for. Only I part company with it when force is called to aid for achieving it. We are all born equal, but we have all these centuries resisted the will of God. The idea of inequality, of 'high and low', is an evil, but I do not believe in eradicating evil from the human breast at the point of the bayonet. The human breast does not lend itself to that means.

H, 13 March 1937

AUGUST 25

Every man has an equal right to the necessaries of life even as birds and beasts have. And since every right carries with it a corresponding duty and the corresponding remedy for resisting any attack upon it, it is merely a matter of finding out the corresponding duties and remedies to vindicate the elementary fundamental equality. The corresponding duty is to labour with my limbs and the corresponding remedy is to non-co-operate with him who deprives me of the fruit of my labour.

YI, 26 March 1931

AUGUST 26

The true source of rights is duty. If we all discharge our duties, rights will not be far to seek. If leaving duties unperformed we run after rights, they escape us like a will-o'-the-wisp. The more we pursue them, the farther they fly. The same teaching has been embodied by Krishna in the immortal words: 'Action alone is thine; leave thou the fruit severely alone.' Action is duty; fruit is the right.

YI, 8 Jan. 1925

AUGUST 27

Let labour realize its dignity and strength. Capital has neither dignity nor strength, compared to labour. These the man in the street also has. In a well-ordered democratic society there is no room, no occasion for lawlessness or strikes. In such a society there are ample lawful means for vindicating justice. Violence, veiled or unveiled, must be taboo.

DD, p. 381

AUGUST 28

Capital controlled labour because it knew the art of combination. Drops in separation would only fade away; drops in co-operation made the ocean which carried on its broad bosom ocean greyhounds. Similarly if all labourers in any part of the world combined together they could not be tempted by higher wages or helplessly allow themselves to be attracted for, say, a pittance.

H, 7 Sept. 1947

AUGUST 29

A true and non-violent combination of labour would act like a magnet attracting to it all the needed capital. Capitalists would then exist only as trustees. When that happy day dawned, there would be no difference between capital and labour. The labour will have ample food, good and sanitary dwellings, all the necessary education for their children, ample leisure for self-education and proper medical assistance.

H, 7 Sept. 1947

AUGUST 30

America is the most industrialized country in the world and yet it has not banished poverty and degradation. That

89

was because it neglected the universal man-power and concentrated power in the hands of the few who amassed fortunes at the expense of the many. The result is that its industrialization has become a menace to its own poor and to the rest of the world.

H, 9 March 1947

AUGUST 31

If India was to escape such a disaster, it had to imitate what was best in America and other western countries and leave aside its attractive-looking but destructive economic policies. Therefore, real planning consisted in the best utilization of the whole manpower of India and the distribution of the raw products of India in her numerous villages instead of sending them outside and re-buying finished articles at fabulous prices.

H, 23 March 1947

SEPTEMBER 1

Daridranarayana is one of the millions of names by which humanity knows God, who is unnamable and unfathomable by human understanding, and it means God of the poor, God appearing in the hearts of the poor.

YI, 4 April 1929

SEPTEMBER 2

I recognize no God except the God that is to be found in the hearts of the dumb millions. They do not recognize his presence; I do. And, I worship the God that is Truth or Truth which is God, through the service of these millions.

H, 11 March 1939

SEPTEMBER 3

For the poor the economic is the spiritual. You cannot make any other appeal to those starving millions. It will fall flat on them. But you take food to them and they will regard you as their God. They are incapable of any other thought.

YI, 5 May 1927

SEPTEMBER 4

With this very hand I have collected soiled pies from them tied tightly in their rags. Talk to them of modern progress. Insult them by taking the name of God before them in vain. They will call you and me fiends if we talk about God to them. They know, if they know any God at all, a God of terror, vengeance, a pitiless tyrant.

YI, 15 Sept. 1927

SEPTEMBER 5

If I preach against the modern artificial life of sensual enjoyment, and ask men and women to go back to the simple life epitomized in the Charkha, I do so because I know that without an intelligent return to simplicity, there is no escape from our descent to a state lower than brutality.

YI, 21 July 1921

SEPTEMBER 6

Don't be dazzled by the splendour that comes to you from the west. Do not be thrown off your feet by this passing show. The Enlightened One has told you in never-to-be-forgotten words that this little span of life is but a passing shadow, a fleeting thing, and if you realize the nothingness of all that appears before your eyes, the nothingness of this material case that we see before us ever changing, then indeed there are treasures for you up above, and there is peace for you down here, peace which passeth all understanding, and happiness to which we are utter strangers. It requires an amazing faith, a divine faith and surrender of all that we see before us.

YI, 8 Dec. 1927

SEPTEMBER 7

What did Buddha do, and Christ do, and also Mohammed? Theirs were lives of self-sacrifice and renunciation. Buddha renounced every worldly happiness because he wanted to share with the whole world, his happiness which was to be had by man who sacrificed and suffered in search for Truth.

Ibid.

SEPTEMBER 8

If it was a good thing to scale the heights of Mt. Ever est, sacrificing precious lives in order to be able to get there and make some slight observations, if it was a glorious thing to give up life after life in planting a flag in the uttermost extremities of the earth, how much more glorious would it be to give not one life, surrender not a million lives but a billion lives in search of the potent and imperishable truth?

YI, 8 Dec. 1927

SEPTEMBER 9

A time is coming when those, who are in the mad rush today of multiplying their wants vainly thinking that they add to the real substance, real knowledge of the world, will retrace their steps and say: 'What have we done?'

Ibid.

SEPTEMBER 10

Civilizations have come and gone, and in spite of all our vaunted progress I am tempted to ask again and again, 'To what purpose?' Wallace, a contemporary of Darwin, has said the same thing. Fifty years of brilliant inventions and discoveries, he has said, has not added one inch to the moral height of mankind. So said a dreamer and visionary if you will,—Tolstoy. So said Jesus, and Buddha, and Mohammed, whose religion is being denied and falsified in my own country today.

YI, 8 Dec. 1927

SEPTEMBER 11

By all means drink deep of the fountains that are given to you in the Sermon on the Mount, but then you will have to take to sackcloth and ashes. The teaching of the Sermon was meant for each and every one of us. You cannot serve both God and Mammon. God the Compassionate and the

Merciful, Tolerance incarnate, allows Mammon to have his nine days' wonder. But I say to you: fly from that self-destroying but destructive show of Mammon.

Ibid.

SEPTEMBER 12

India's destiny lies not along the bloody way of the West, of which she shows signs of tiredness, but along the bloodless way of peace that comes from a simple and godly life. India is in danger of losing her soul. She cannot lose it and live. She must not therefore lazily and helplessly say: 'I cannot escape the onrush from the West.' She must be strong enough to resist it for her own sake and that of the world.

YI, 7 Oct. 1926

SEPTEMBER 13

I do believe, that if India had patience enough to go through the fire of suffering and to resist any unlawful encroachment upon its own civilization which, imperfect though it undoubtedly is, has hitherto stood the ravages of time, she can make a lasting contribution to the peace and solid progress of the world.

YI, 11 Aug. 1927

SEPTEMBER 14

I feel that India's mission is different from that of others. India is fitted for the religious supremacy of the world. There is no parallel in the world for the process of purification that this country has voluntarily undergone.

SW, p. 405

SEPTEMBER 15

India is essentially *karmabhumi* ·(land of duty) in contradiction to *bhogabhumi* (land of enjoyment).

YI, 5 Feb. 1925

SEPTEMBER 16

India has never waged war against any nation. She has put up sometimes ill-organized or half-organized resistance in self-defence pure and simple. She has, therefore, not got to develop the will for peace. She has that in abundance whether she knows it or not.

YI, 4 July 1929

SEPTEMBER 17

I want India to recognize that she has a soul that cannot perish and that can rise triumphant above every physical weakness and defy the physical combination of a whole world.

YI, 11 Aug. 1920

SEPTEMBER 18

I venture to suggest, in all humility, that if India reaches her destiny through truth and non-violence, she will have made no small contribution to the world peace for which all the nations of the earth are thirsting and she would also have, in that case, made some slight return for the help that those nations have been freely giving to her.

YI, 12 March 1921

SEPTEMBER 19

India's freedom must revolutionize the world's outlook upon peace and war. Her impotence affects the whole of mankind.

YI, 17 Sept. 1925

SEPTEMBER 20

Our nationalism can be no peril to other nations inasmuch as we will exploit none, just as we will allow none to exploit us. Through Swaraj we will serve the whole world.

YI, 16 April 1931

SEPTEMBER 21

If the mad race for armaments continues it is bound to result in a slaughter such as has never occurred in history. If there is a victor left the very victory will be a living death for the nation that emerges victorious.

H, 12 Nov. 1938

SEPTEMBER 22

There is no escape from the impending doom save through a bold and unconditional acceptance of the non-violent method with all its glorious implications.

Ibid.

SEPTEMBER 23

If there were no greed, there would be no occasion for armaments. The principle of non-violence necessitates complete abstention from exploitation in any form.

H, 12 Nov. 1938

September 24

Immediately the spirit of exploitation is gone, armaments will be felt as a positive unbearable burden. Real disarmament cannot come unless the nations of the world cease to exploit one another.

Ibid.

September 25

The better mind of the world desires today not absolutely independent States warring one against another, but a federation of friendly interdependent States.

YI, 26 Dec. 1924

September 26

Interdependence is and ought to be as much the ideal of man as self-sufficiency. Man is a social being. Without interrelation with society he cannot realize its oneness with the universe or suppress his egotism.

YI, 21 March 1929

September 27

His social interdependence enables him to test his faith and to prove himself on the touchstone of reality. If man were so placed or could so place himself as to be absolutely above all dependence on his fellow-beings he would become so proud and arrogant as to be a veritable burden and nuisance to the world.

Ibid.

SEPTEMBER 28

Dependence on society teaches him the lesson of humility. That a man ought to be able to satisfy most of his essential needs himself is obvious; but it is no less obvious to me when self-sufficiency is carried to the length of isolating oneself from society it almost amounts to sin.

Ibid.

SEPTEMBER 29

It is impossible for one to be internationalist without being a nationalist. Internationalism is possible only when nationalism becomes a fact, i.e., when peoples belonging to different countries have organized themselves and are able to act as one man.

YI, 18 June 1925

September 30

It is not nationalism that is evil, it is the narrowness, selfishness, exclusiveness which is the bane of modern nations which is evil. Each wants to profit at the expense of, and rise on the ruin of, the other.

Ibid.

October 1

A large part of the miseries of today can be avoided, if we look at the relations between the sexes in a healthy and pure light, and regard ourselves as trustees for the moral welfare of the future generations.

YI, 27 Sept. 1928

October 2

What chiefly distinguishes man from the beast is that man from his age of discretion begins to practise a life of continual self-restraint. God has enabled man to distinguish between the sister, his mother, his daughter and his wife.

WGC, p. 84

October 3

Human society is a ceaseless growth, an unfoldment in terms of spirituality. If

so, it must be based on ever increasing
restraint upon the demands of the flesh.
Thus, marriage must be considered to be a
sacrament imposing discipline upon the
partners, restricting them to the physical
union only among themselves and for the
purpose only of procreation when both the
partners desire and are prepared for it.

YI, 16 Sept. 1926

OCTOBER 4

Sex urge is a fine and noble thing.
There is nothing to be ashamed of in it.
But it is meant only for the act of creation.
Any other use of it is a sin against God and
humanity.

H, 28 March 1936

OCTOBER 5

Absolute renunciation, absolute *brahmacharya*, is the ideal state. If you dare not
think of it, marry by all means, but even
then live a life of self-control.

H, 7 Sept. 1935

OCTOBER 6

Marriage is a natural thing in life, and
to consider it derogatory in any sense is

wholly wrong. . . .The ideal is to look upon marriage as a sacrament, and therefore, to lead a life of self-restraint in the married estate.

H, 22 March 1942

OCTOBER 7

Brahmacharya is not mere mechanical celibacy, it means complete control over all the senses and freedom from lust in thought, word and deed. As such it is the royal road to self-realization or attainment of Brahman.

YI, 29 April 1926

OCTOBER 8

Marriage is meant to cleanse the hearts of the couple of sordid passion and take them nearer god. Lustless love between husband and wife is not impossible. Man is not a brute. He has risen to a higher state after countless births in the brute creation. He is born to stand, not to walk on all fours or crawl. Bestiality is as far removed from manhood as matter from spirit.

Ibid.

OCTOBER 9

The wife is not the husband's bondslave but his companion and his help-mate and an

equal partner in all his joys and sorrows
—as free as the husband to choose her
own path.

Auto, p. 25

OCTOBER 10

You will guard your wife's honour and
be not her master, but her true friend. You
will hold her body and her soul as sacred
as I trust she will hold your body and your
soul. To that end you will have to live a
life of prayerful toil, and simplicity and self-
restraint. Let not either of you regard
another as the object of his or her lust.

YI, 2 Feb. 1928

OCTOBER 11

Just as fundamentally man and woman
are one, their problem must be one in
essence. The soul in both is the same. The
two live the same life, have the same
feelings. Each is a complement of the other.
The one cannot live without the other's
active help.

H, 24 Feb. 1940

OCTOBER 12

But somehow or other man has domi-
nated woman from ages past, and so woman

has developed an inferiority complex. She
has believed in the truth of man's interested
teaching that she is inferior to him. But
seers among men have recognized her
equal status.

H, 24 Feb. 1940

OCTOBER 13

Nevertheless there is no doubt that at
some point there is bifurcation. Whilst
both are fundamentally one, it is also equally
true that in that form there is a vital difference between the two. Hence the voca-
tions of the two must also be different. The
duty of motherhood, which the vast majority of women will always undertake, requires qualities which man need not possess. She is passive, he is active. She is essentially mistress of the house. He is the
bread-winner. She is the keeper and dis-
tributor of the bread. She is the care-
taker in every sense of the term.

Ibid.

OCTOBER 14

Woman is the companion of man,
gifted with equal mental capacities. She has
the right to participate in very minutest

105

detail in the activities of man and she has
an equal right of freedom and liberty with
him.

SW, p. 425

OCTOBER 15

Of all the evils for which man has
made himself responsible, none is so degrad-
ing, so shocking or so brutal as his abuse
of the better half of humanity to me, the
female sex, not the weaker sex. It is the
nobler of the two, for it is even today the
embodiment of sacrifice, silent suffering,
humility, faith and knowledge.

YI, 15 Sept. 1921

OCTOBER 16

Woman, I hold, is the personification
of self-sacrifice, but unfortunately today
she does not realize what a tremendous
advantage she has over man. As Tolstoy
used to say, they are labouring under the
hypnotic influence of man. If they would
realize the strength of non-violence they
would not consent to be called the weaker
sex.

YI, 14 Jan. 1932

OCTOBER 17

Man has regarded woman as his tool. She has learnt to be his tool, and in the end found this easy and comfortable to be such, because when one drags another in his fall the descent is easy.

H, 25 Jan. 1936

OCTOBER 18

Woman must cease to consider herself the object of man's lust. The remedy is more in her hands than man's. She must refuse to adorn herself for men, including her husband, if she will be an equal partner with man. I cannot imagine Sita ever wasting a single moment on pleasing Rama by physical charms.

YI, 21 July 1921

OCTOBER 19

Women are special custodians of all that is pure and religious in life. Conservative by nature, if they are slow to shed superstitious habits, they are also slow to give up all that is pure and noble in life.

H, 25 March 1933

Woman is the incarnation of Ahimsa. Ahimsa means infinite love, which again means infinite capacity for suffering. Who but woman, the mother of man, shows this capacity in the largest measure? She shows it as she carries the infant and feeds it during nine months and derives joy in the suffering involved. What can beat the suffering involved by the pangs of labour? But she forgets them in the joy of creation. Who, again, suffers daily so that her babe may wax from day to day? Let her transfer that love to the whole of humanity, let her forget that she was or can be the object of man's lust. And she will occupy her proud position by the side of man as his mother, maker and silent leader. It is given to her to teach the art of peace to the warring world thirsting for that nectar.

H, 24 Feb. 1940

There is as much reason for man to wish that he was born a woman as for woman to do otherwise. But the wish is fruitless. Let us be happy in the state to which we are born and do the duty for which nature has destined us.

Ibid.

OCTOBER 22

Chastity is not a hot-house growth. It cannot be protected by the surrounding wall of the purdah. It must grow from within, and to be worth anything it must be capable of withstanding unsought temptation.

YI, 3 Dec. 1927

OCTOBER 23

And why is there all this morbid anxiety about female purity? Have women any say in the matter of male purity? We hear nothing of women's anxiety about men's chastity. Why should men arrogate to themselves the right to regulate female purity? It cannot be superimposed from without. It is a matter of evolution from within and therefore of individual self-effort.

YI, 25 Nov. 1926

OCTOBER 24

It is my firm conviction that a fearless woman who knows that her purity is her best shield can never be dishonoured. However beastly the man, he will bow in shame before the flame of her dazzling purity.

H, 1 March 1942

OCTOBER 25

Let it be man's privilege to protect woman, but let no woman of India feel helpless in the absence of man or in the event of his failing to perform the sacred duty of protecting her. One who knows how to die need never fear any harm to her or his honour.

YI, 15 Dec. 1921

OCTOBER 26

Man must choose either of the two courses, the upward or the downward; but as he has the brute in him, he will more easily choose the downward course than the upward, especially when the downward course is presented to him in a beautiful garb. Man easily capitulates when sin is presented in the garb of virtue.

H, 21 Jan. 1935

OCTOBER 27

It is wrong and immoral to seek to escape the consequences of one's acts. It is good for a person who overeats to have an ache and a fast. It is bad for him to indulge his appetite and then escape the consequence by taking tonics or other medicine. It is still worse for a person to indulge in animal passions and escape the consequences of his acts.

YI, 12 March 1925

OCTOBER 28

Nature is relentless and will have full revenge for any such violation of her laws. Moral results can only be produced by moral restraints. All other restraints defeat the very purpose for which they are intended.

Ibid.

OCTOBER 29

The world depends for its existence on the act of generation, and as the world is the playground of God and a reflection of His glory, the act of generation should be controlled for the ordered growth of the world.

Auto, p. 204

OCTOBER 30

The conquest of lust is the highest endeavour of a man or woman's existence. Without overcoming lust man cannot hope to rule over self. . . . And without rule over self there can be no Swaraj or *Ramaraj*. Rule of all without rule of oneself would prove to be as deceptive and disappointing as a painted toy-mango, charming to look at outwardly but hollow and empty within.

H, 21 Nov. 1936

OCTOBER 31

The ideal that marriage aims at is that of spiritual union through the physical. The human love that it incarnates is intended to serve as a stepping stone to divine or universal love.

YI, 21 May 1931

NOVEMBER 1

It is not man's duty to develop *all* his faculties to perfection: his duty is to develop all his God-ward faculties to perfection and to suppress completely those of contrary tendencies.

YI, 24 June 1926

November 2

Man is neither mere intellect, nor the gross animal body, nor the heart or soul alone. A proper and harmonious combination of all the three is required for the making of the whole man and constitutes the true economics of education.

H, 11 Sept. 1937

November 3

I hold that true education of the intellect can only come through a proper exercise and training of the bodily organs, e.g., hands, feet, eyes, ears, nose, etc. In other words, an intelligent use of the bodily organs in a child provides the best and quickest way of developing his intellect.

H, 8 March 1937

November 4

But unless the development of the mind and body goes hand in hand with a corresponding awakening of the soul, the former alone would prove to be a poor lop-sided affair. By spiritual training I mean education of the heart. A proper and all-round development of the mind, therefore, can take place only when it proceeds *pari passu* with the education of the physical and spiritual faculties of the child. They constitute an indivisible whole.

H, 17 April 1937

NOVEMBER 5

In my scheme of things the hand will handle tools before it draws or traces the writing. The eyes will read the pictures of letters and words as they will know other things in life, the ears will catch the names and meanings of things and sentences. The whole training will be natural, responsive and, therefore, the quickest and the cheapest in the world.

H, 28 Aug. 1937

NOVEMBER 6

Literary education should follow the education of the hand — the one gift that visibly distinguishes man from the beast. It is a superstition to think that the fullest development of man is impossible without a knowledge of the art of reading and writing. That knowledge undoubtedly adds grace to life, but is in no way indispensable for man's moral, physical or material growth.

H, 8 March 1935

November 7

The introduction of manual training will serve a double purpose in a poor country like ours. It will pay for the education of our children and teach them an occupation, on which they can fall back in after life, if they choose, for earning a living. Such a system must make our children self-reliant. Nothing will demoralize the nation so much as that we should learn to despise labour.

YI, 1 Sept. 1926

November 8

Among the many evils of foreign rule, this blighting imposition of a foreign medium upon the youth of the country will be counted by history as one of the greatest. It has sapped the energy of the nation, it has shortened the lives of the pupils. It has estranged them from the masses, it has made education unnecessarily expensive. If this process is still persisted in, it bids fair to rob the nation of its soul.

YI, 5 July 1928

November 9

If we are to reach real peace in this world and if we are to carry on a real war against war, we shall have to begin with children; and if they will grow up in their natural innocence, we won't have to struggle; we won't have to pass fruitless idle resolutions, but we shall go from love to love and peace to peace, until at last all the corners of the world are covered with that peace and love for which consciously or unconsciously the whole world is hungering.

YI, 19 Nov. 1931

NOVEMBER 10

Real education consists in drawing the best out of yourself. What better book can there be than the book of humanity?

H, 30 March 1934

NOVEMBER 11

A nation-building programme can leave no part of the nation untouched. Students have to react upon the dumb millions. They have to learn to think, not in terms of a province, or a town, or a class or a caste, but in terms of a continent and of the millions who include untouchables, drunkards, hooligans and even prostitutes, for whose existence in our midst every one of us is responsible.

YI, 9 June 1927

NOVEMBER 12

Students in olden times were called *brahmacharis*, i.e., those who walked with and in the fear of God. They were honoured by kings and elders. They were a voluntary charge on the nation, and in turn they gave to the nation a hundred-fold strong souls, strong brains, strong arms.

Ibid.

NOVEMBER 13

All true art is an expression of the soul. The outward forms have value only in so far as they are expression of the inward spirit of man.

YI, 13 Nov. 1924

NOVEMBER 14

What conscious art of man can give me the panoramic scenes that open out before me, when I look up to the sky above with all its shining stars? This, however, does not mean that I refuse to accept the value of productions of art, generally accepted as such, but only that I personally feel how inadequate these are compared with the eternal symbols of beauty in Nature. These productions of man's art have their value only in so far as they help the soul onward towards self-realization.

YI, 13 Nov. 1924

NOVEMBER 15

To a true artist only that face is beautiful which, quite apart from its exterior, shines with the Truth within the soul. There is . . . no Beauty apart from Truth. On the other hand, Truth may manifest itself in forms which may not be outwardly beautiful at all.

Ibid.

NOVEMBER 16

I see and find Beauty in Truth or through Truth. All Truth, not merely true ideas but truthful faces, truthful pictures, or songs are highly beautiful. People generally fail to see Beauty in Truth, the ordinary man runs away from and becomes blind to the Beauty in it. Whenever men begin to see Beauty in Truth, then true art will arise.

YI, 13 Nov. 1924

NOVEMBER 17

When I admire the wonder of a sunset
or the beauty of the moon, my soul expands
in worship of the Creator. I try to see Him
and His mercies in all these creations. But
even the sunsets and sunrises would be
mere hindrances if they did not help me
to think of Him. Anything, which is a
hindrance to the flight of the soul, is a
delusion and a snare; even like the body,
which often does actually hinder you in
the path of salvation.

Ibid.

NOVEMBER 18

Life is greater than all art. I would go
even further and declare that the man
whose life comes nearest to perfection is the
greatest artist; for what is art without the
sure foundation and framework of a noble
life?

LG, p. 210

NOVEMBER 19

After all true art can only be expressed
not through inanimate power-driven
machinery designed for mass production,

but only through the delicate living touch of the hands of men and women.

YI, 13 March 1929

NOVEMBER 20

True art takes note not merely of form but also of what lies behind. There is an art that kills and an art that gives life. True art must be evidence of happiness, contentment and purity of its authors.

YI, 11 Aug. 1921

NOVEMBER 21

Purity of life is the highest and truest art. The art of producing good music from a cultivated voice can be achieved by many, but the art of producing that music from the harmony of a pure life is achieved very rarely.

H, 19 Feb. 1938

NOVEMBER 22

No culture can live, if it attempts to be exclusive. There is no such thing as pure Aryan culture in existence today in India. Whether the Aryans were indigenous to India or were unwelcome visitors, does not interest me much. What does interest me is the fact that my remote ancestors blended with one another with the utmost freedom and we of the present generation are a result of that blend. Whether we are doing any good to the country of our birth and the tiny globe that sustains us or whether we are a burden, the future alone will show.

H, 9 May 1936

NOVEMBER 23

I am no indiscriminate superstitious worshipper of all that goes under the name of 'ancient'. I never hesitated to endeavour to demolish all that is evil or immoral, no matter how ancient it may be, but with this reservation. I must confess to you that I am an adorer of ancient institutions and it hurts me to think that people in their mad rush for everything modern despise all their ancient traditions and ignore them in their lives.

WGC, p. 105

NOVEMBER 24

We have to decide whether we shall indiscriminately copy this civilization. We may well pause in the face of the awful revelations that come to us from the West from time to time, and ask ourselves, whether after all it is not better to hold by our own civilization and seek in the light of the comparative knowledge that is available to us, to reform it by removing its known excrescences.

YI, 2 June 1927

NOVEMBER 25

It is perhaps unnecessary, if not useless, to weigh the merits of the two civilizations. It is likely that the West has evolved a civilization suited to its climate and surroundings and similarly, we have a civilization suited to our conditions and both are good in their own respective spheres.

YI, 2 June 1927

NOVEMBER 26

Cowardliness which often springs from pacific training, and obsequiousness which comes from the restraint that is handed down from generation to generation, have somehow to be avoided, if the ancient civilization is not to perish before the mad modern rush.

Ibid.

November 27

The distinguishing characteristic of modern civilization is an indefinite multiplicity of human wants. The characteristic of ancient civilization is an imperative restriction upon and a strict regulating of these wants.

Ibid.

November 28

The modern or Western insatiableness arises really from want of a living faith in a future state and therefore also in Divinity. The restraint of ancient or Eastern civilization arises from a belief, often in spite of ourselves, in a future state and the existence of a Divine Power.

YI, 2 June 1927

November 29

Some of the immediate and brilliant results of modern inventions are too maddening to resist. But I have no manner of doubt that the victory of man lies in that resistance. We are in danger of bartering away the permanent good for a momentary pleasure.

Ibid.

November 30

I do not want my house to be walled in on all sides and my windows to be stuffed. I want the cultures of all the lands to be blown about my house as freely as possible. But I refuse to be blown off my feet by any. I refuse to live in other people's houses as an interloper, a beggar or a slave.

YI, 1 June 1921

December 1

Democracy must in essence mean the art and science of mobilizing the entire physical, economic and spiritual resources of all the various sections of the people in the service of the common good of all.

H, 27 May 1939

December 2

A born democrat is a born disciplinarian. Democracy comes naturally to him who is habituated normally to yield willing obedience to all laws, human or divine.

Ibid.

December 3

Willing submission to social restraint for the sake of the well-being of the whole society enriches both the individual and the society of which one is a member.

Ibid.

DECEMBER 4

The spirit of democracy is not a mechanical thing to be adjusted by abolition of forms. It requires change of the heart.

YI, 16 March 1927

DECEMBER 5

The spirit of democracy cannot be established in the midst of terrorism whether governmental or popular. In some respects popular terrorism is more antagonistic to the growth of the democratic spirit than the governmental. For the latter strengthens the spirit of democracy, whereas the former kills it.

YI, 23 Feb. 1921

DECEMBER 6

Democracy disciplined and enlightened is the finest thing in the world. A democracy, prejudiced, ignorant, superstitious will land itself in chaos and may be self-destroyed.

YI, 30 July 1931

December 7

The democracy of my conception is wholly inconsistent with the use of physical force for enforcing its will.

EF, p. 102

December 8

Democracy will break under the strain of apron strings. It can exist only on trust.

DD, p. 136

December 9

The highest form of freedom carries with it the greatest measure of discipline and humility. Freedom that comes from discipline and humility cannot be denied; unbridled licence is a sign of vulgarity, injurious alike to self and one's neighbours.

YI, 3 June 1926

December 10

When people come into possession of political powers, the interference with the freedom of the people is reduced to a minimum. In other words, a nation that runs its affairs smoothly and effectively without such State interference is truly democratic.

Where such a condition is absent, the form of Government is democratic in name.

H, 11 Jan. 1936

DECEMBER 11

Democracy and violence can ill go together. The States that are today nominally democratic have either to become frankly totalitarian or, if they are to become truly democratic, they must become courageously non-violent. It is a blasphemy to say that non-violence can only be practised by individuals and never by nations which are composed of individuals.

H, 12 Nov. 1938

DECEMBER 12

The true democrat is he who with purely non-violent means defends his liberty and, therefore, his country's and ultimately that of the whole of mankind.

H, 15 April 1939

DECEMBER 13

In matters of conscience, the Law of Majority has no place.

YI, 4 Aug. 1920

DECEMBER 14

Let us not push the mandate theory to ridiculous extremes and become slave to resolutions of majorities. That would be a revival of brute force in a more virulent form. If rights of minorities are to be respected, the majority must tolerate and respect their opinion and action.... It will be the duty of the majority to see to it that the minorities receive a proper hearing and are not otherwise exposed to insults.

YI, 8 Dec. 1921

DECEMBER 15

The rule of majority has a narrow application, i.e., one should yield to the majority in matters of detail. But it is slavery to be amenable to the majority, no matter what its decisions are.

YI, 2 March 1922

DECEMBER 16

Democracy is not a state in which people act like sheep. Under democracy, individual liberty of opinion and action is jealously guarded. I, therefore, believe that the minority has a perfect right to act differently from the majority.

Ibid.

DECEMBER 17

Keep a child in cotton wools and stunt it or kill it. If you will let it develop into a robust man, you will expose his body to all weathers teaching him how to defy them. Precisely in the same manner, a government worth the name has to show the nation how to face deficits, bad weathers and other handicaps of life through its own collective effort instead of its being effortlessly helped to live anyhow.

DD, p. 242

DECEMBER 18

Possession of power makes men blind and deaf, they cannot see things which are under their very nose and cannot hear things which invade their ears. There is thus no knowing what power-intoxicated government may not do. So. . . patriotic men ought to be prepared for death, imprisonment and similar eventualities.

YI, 13 Oct. 1921

DECEMBER 19

Power that comes from service faithfully rendered ennobles. Power that is sought in the name of service and can only be obtained by a majority of votes is a delusion and a snare to be avoided.

YI, 11 Sept. 1924

DECEMBER 20

Power is of two kinds. One is obtained by the fear of punishment and the other by arts of love. Power based on love is a thousand times more effective and permanent than the one derived from fear of punishment.

YI, 8 Jan. 1925

DECEMBER 21

Whilst power, superimposed, always needs the help of police and military, power generated from within should have little or no use for them.

H, 4 Sept. 1937

DECEMBER 22

Those who claim to lead the masses must resolutely refuse to be led by them, if we want to avoid mob law and desire ordered progress for the country. I believe that mere protestation of one's opinion and surrender

130

to the mass opinion is not only not enough, but in matters of vital importance, leaders must *act* contrary to the mass opinion if it does not commend itself to their reason.

YI, 14 July 1920

DECEMBER 23

Love and Ahimsa are matchless in their effect. But, in their play there is no fuss, show, noise or placards. They presuppose self-confidence which in its turn presupposes self-purification. Men of stainless character and self-purification will easily inspire confidence and automatically purify the atmosphere around them.

YI, 6 Sept. 1928

DECEMBER 24

The reformer's path is strewn not with roses, but with thorns, and he has to walk warily. He can but limp, dare not jump.

YI, 28 Nov. 1929

DECEMBER 25

The only code that guides a reformer is his own conscience in the last resort. . . . The law would be corrected through the righteous suffering of a few if public opinion had not already secured either correction or disuse.

YI, 7 Feb. 1929

DECEMBER 26

All is well with you even though everything seems to go dead wrong, if you are square with yourself. Reversely, all is not well with you although everything outwardly may seem to go right, if you are not square with yourself.

H, 20 May 1939

DECEMBER 27

My patriotism is not an exclusive thing. It is all-embracing and I should reject that patriotism which sought to mount upon the distress of the exploitation of other nationalities. The conception of my patriotism is nothing if it is not always, in every case, without exception, consistent with the broadest good of humanity at large.

YI, 4 April 1929

DECEMBER 28

I do not believe . . . that an individual may gain spiritually and those who surround him suffer. I believe in *advaita*, I believe in the essential unity of man and for that matter, of all that lives. Therefore, I believe that if one man gains spiritually, the whole world gains with him and if one man falls the whole world falls to that extent.

YI, 4 Dec. 1924

DECEMBER 29

Mankind is one, seeing that all are equally subject to the moral law. All men are equal in God's eyes. There are, of course, differences of race and status and the like, but the higher the status of man, the greater is his responsibility.

ER, p. 57

DECEMBER 30

Just as the cult of patriotism teaches us today that the individual has to die for the family, the family has to die for the village, the village for the district, the district for the province, and the province for the country, and so a country has to be free in order that it may die, if necessary, for the benefit of the world.

GIV, p. 170

9-5682

DECEMBER 31

A nation that is capable of limitless sacrifice is capable of rising to limitless heights. The purer the sacrifice the quicker the progress.

YI, 25 Aug. 1920